Seven Sacred Stations of the Self & Seven Flaming Fiats of Light upon The Seven Cosmic-Physical Rays

Etbonan Karta

Printed in January 2016 by Marquis Printers

©Seven Sacred Stations of the Self & Seven Flaming Fiats of Light upon the Seven Cosmic-Physical Rays, Etbonan Karta.

ISBN: 978-1-928016-04-5 (1st English edition, 2016)
ISBN: 978-0-9687048-4-4 (1st bilingual edition [English-French] 2001)

**Magnificent
Magus
Publications**

Magnificent Magus Publications©

Registration of copyright: 1st trimester 2016 (1st English edition)
Registration of copyright: 1st trimester 2001 (1st bilingual edition)
National Library of Quebec
National Library of Canada

Magnificent Magus Publications©
1206 Saint-Luc Boulevard, Suite 110
Saint-Jean-sur-Richelieu, Québec, J2Y 1A5, Canada
info@palmpublications.com
www.palmpublications.com

Cover and graphics: Simhananda, Lucie Robitaille
Typesetting: Sareyu Honan Roy, Lucie Létourneau

All rights reserved. No part of this book may be reproduced in any form without permission in writing from the author, except to quote or photocopy specific passages for the purposes of group study.

By the same author

Buddhism:

The Great Golden Garland of Gampopa's Sublime Considerations on the Supreme Path – Contemplative Contemporary Commentaries of Gampopa's Root Text, volumes 1 and 2

Holy-Moly Hiccoughs and Enigmatic Knotty Eructations From the Boffola Belly of Bu'Tai. The Drôleries and Dictums of Crazy Modern Dzog-zen

Contemplative Sayings:

Knots of Eternity – Paradoxes From Dadi to Daughter, volume 1

The Smiling Forehead – Paradoxes from Dadi to Daughter, volume 2

Scriptings of the Soul, In Questions of Light – Simhananda's Little Book of Self-Inquiry

Paradisal Plums: Peaceful Ponderings from a (Rebel) Pandit's Puce Palm – Aphorisms, Adages, and Analects of Sri Adi Dadi, volumes 1 and 2

The Science of Invocation / The Seven Rays:

The Science of Full Moon Invocations – from Humanity's Heart to Hierarchy's Will

Seven Studies of Soul Stations or Soul-ar Progressions Upon Each of the Seven Cosmic-Physical Rays (an integral excerpt from *Collectanea One, The Divine Concordance of Light*)

The Divine Concordance of Light: A Handbook from Heaven to Progression Earth – The Seven Rays of God: Seven Studies of the Soul's Earthly Pilgrimage of Service Upon the Seven Cosmic-Physical Rays

Transformative Photography:

Emaho Tibet, Blessings from the Land of the Snows – A Photographic Pilgrimage of Ongoing Spirituality

Towards A Transformative Photography

Our Ordinary Extraordinary Earth and Its Extraordinary Ordinary People

Touch To This Earth Where Meanders Mankind

Buddhas, Bodhisattvas, Khadromas and the Way of the Pilgrim – A Transformative Book of Photography and Pithy Sayings

Dedicated to the *transformative* and Healing Self
in each and every being.

This book is an integral excerpt taken from *The Divine Concordance of Light: A Handbook from Heaven to Progression Earth* (Addenda II and III) by Etbonan Karta.

Three Progressions of «*Seven Sacred Stations*» of the *Self*,
and Seven «*Flaming Fiats*» of "Light"
(*Declarations, Manifestos, and Healings*) by the Soul
upon Each of the Seven Cosmic-Physical Rays

Foreword

The simple «*Stations*» contained within this book serve to rightly align and gently, (but rootedly), fix the disciple to his Higher Self.

In the process, they also position him in *Sacred-Relatedness* to the mighty expressions of DIVINE RADIATION, both solar and electrical, which are known as the Cosmic-Physical Rays.

The forceful «*Flaming Fiats*» in their turn, act to invoke into the erstwhile student's life a powerful Soul-Resonance; and activate a creative descent of both the positive and healing, *qualitative energies* of the Seven Rays.

In direct proportion to the sadhaka's *Real-Readiness* upon the Path, these unobtrusive «*Stations and Fiats*» act basically, as a Consciousness-catalyzer, thereby leading the seeker on to that high state of Individualized unfoldment known as the Divine Merging of all that is *"Other"*, into SELF.

Consequently, we find revealed within this section a concise and practical form of sacred *asseverations*, reminding the practitioner of both the Basic Unity of all beings and the Divine Confluence of all things.

Note

1. Instead of one's own *SELF,* a brother's Soul-Self may be placed within the *formulae and identified with,* for the selfless purpose of helping and/or healing a particular circumstance, or condition of health.

2. "I" and "my-*SELF*" can be substituted by "We" and "our-*SELF*"; whereas "myself" and "me" may be replaced by their respective plurals, (or Group-consciousness counterparts), that is, "ourselves" and "us".

3. In *Progression Three,* where the subject dealt with is that of HEALING, the **Beneficiary,** that is to say, the NAME of the Person (in need of benefit, nurturing, support, guidance, help or healing, etc.), may be utilized within the "Sacred Stations" format, instead of the usual "my-*SELF*".

The Invoker, however, must endeavor at each station to call in, or always try to contact the **Beneficiary's** Inner Self, or Soul.

The "Flaming Fiat" that is found at the end of each "Sacred Station" must be recited dynamically... with the Invoker identifying fully with the **Beneficiary...** as if he, (or she), was reciting it through his, (or her), *SELF.*

Progression One

«*Seven Sacred Stations*» of the *Self*, and
Seven «*Flaming Fiats*» of "Light" *Declarations* by the Soul
upon Each of the Seven Cosmic-Physical Rays

«S.S.S.» 1 to 7

«F.F.»   1 to 7

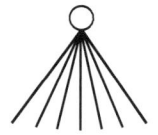

« S.S.S. » One
Upon Ray I
"The SELF and the *Liberating* Light"

I place my-*SELF*,

In the Lord's *Liberating* Light

Under the Lightning Direction

Of the Finger of God.

« F.F. » 1

**« I proclaim myself as Light and
I declare myself to be Free! »**

« S.S.S. » Two
Upon Ray II
"The SELF and the *Saving* Light"

I place my-SELF,

In the Lord's *Saving* Light

Within the Radiant Garden

Of the Cosmic Christ.

« F.F. » 2

**« I maintain myself as Light and
I submit myself as Saved! »**

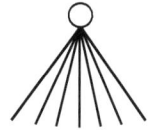

« S.S.S. » Three
Upon Ray III
"The SELF and the *Intelligent* Light"

I place my-*SELF*,

In the Lord's *Intelligent* Light

Under the Active Evolution

Of the Universal Mind.

« F.F. » 3

**« I posit myself as Light manifest and
I propose that I am Intelligence incarnate! »**

« S.S.S. » Four
Upon Ray IV
"The SELF and the *Melodious* Light"

I place my-*SELF*,

In the Lord's *Melodious* Light

Under the Symmetrical Concord

Of the Hidden One.

« F.F. » 4

« I herald myself as Light and
I hold to my heart the Harmony of God! »

« S.S.S. » Five
Upon Ray V
"The SELF and the *Revealing* Light"

I place my-*SELF*,

In the Lord's *Revealing* Light

Under the Knowledgeable Mastership

Of the Fifth Guardian.

« F.F. » 5

**« I predicate myself as Light and
I base my knowledge upon the Lord's Revelation! »**

«S.S.S.» Six
Upon Ray VI
"The SELF and the *Visionary* Light"

I place my-*SELF*,

In the Lord's *Visionary* Light

Under the Devoted Tutorship

Of the Imperishable One.

«F.F.» 6

«I profess myself to be made of Pure Light and I build my Foundation upon my Godly Vision!»

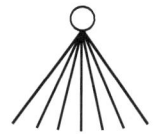

« S.S.S. » Seven
Upon Ray VII
"The Self and the *Unveiling* Light"

I place my-*Self*,

In the Lord's *Unveiling* Light

Under the Magical Rhythm

Of the Alchemist Divine.

« F.F. » 7

« I create myself *magically* as an expression of Divine Light and I enunciate the Mystery of God in the Lord's unveiling of my-Self! »

Progression Two

«*Seven Sacred Stations*» of the *Self*, and
Seven «*Flaming Fiats*» of "Light" *Manifestos* by the Soul
upon Each of the Seven Cosmic-Physical Rays

«S.S.S.» **8 to 14**

«F.F.»   **8 to 14**

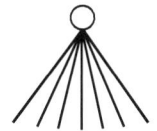

« S.S.S. » Eight
Upon Ray I
"The SELF and the *Dynamic* Direction"

I place my-*SELF*,

In the Lord's Powerful Light

Under the *Dynamic* Direction

Of the Burning Breath.

« F.F. » 8

« Know that I am the Light of *LIFE* Itself! »

« S.S.S. » Nine
Upon Ray II
"The Self and the *Compassionate* Garden"

I place my-*Self*,

In the Lord's Wisdom Light

Within the *Compassionate* Garden

Of the Lord of Love.

« F.F. » 9

« **Know that I am the Light of *Love* Itself!** »

« S.S.S. » Ten
Upon Ray III
"The SELF and the *Adaptive* Evolution"

I place my-*SELF*,

In the Lord's Network of Light

Under the *Adaptive* Evolution

Of the Wick of Truth.

« F.F. » 10

« Know that I am the Light of *MIND* Itself! »

« S.S.S. » Eleven
Upon Ray IV
"The Self and the *Corrective* Concord"

I place my-*Self*,

In the Lord's Sweet-Sounding, Rolling Light

Under the *Corrective* Concord

Of the Hand of Love.

« F.F. » 11

« Know that I am the Light of the *Verb* Itself! »

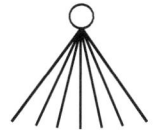

« S.S.S. » Twelve
Upon Ray V
"The SELF and the *Scientific* Mastership"

I place my-*SELF*,

In the Lord's Purifying Light

Under the *Scientific* Mastership

Of the Angel of the Flaming Sword.

« F.F. » 12

« Know that I am the Light of *KNOWLEDGE* Itself! »

« S.S.S. » Thirteen
Upon Ray VI
"The SELF and the *Sacrificial* Tutorship"

I place my-*SELF*,

In the Lord's Fearless Light

Under the *Sacrificial* Tutorship

Of the Lord of Right.

« F.F. » 13

« Know that I am the D. Light of *IDEALISM* Itself! »

*D.: Devotional

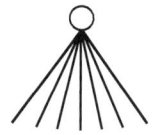

« S.S.S. » Fourteen
Upon Ray VII
"The SELF and the *Creative* Rhythm"

I place my-*SELF*,

In the Lord's Synthesizing Light

Under the *Creative* Rhythm

Of the Square Builder.

« F.F. » 14

« Know that I am the Light (*of the Magic*) of *CREATION* Itself! »

Progression Three

«*Seven Sacred Stations*» of the *Self*, and
Seven «*Flaming Fiats*» of "Light" *Healings* by the Soul
upon Each of the Seven Cosmic-Physical Rays

«S.S.S.» 15 to 21

«F.F.»   15 to 21

« S.S.S. » Fifteen
Upon Ray I
"The Self and the *Most High One*"

I place my-*Self*,

In the Lord's Clear Light

Under the Detached Direction

Of the *Most High One*.

« F.F. » 15

**« I Am That I Am the Light and because
I Am That — I am *healed!* »**

«S.S.S.» Sixteen
Upon Ray II
"The SELF and the *Master Builder*"

I place my-*SELF*,

In the Lord's Renewing Light

In the Expansive Garden

Of the *Master Builder*.

«F.F.» 16

«I Am the Light of the Christ which Is in me
and with His All-Seeing Eye,
I envision myself — as *healed!*»

« S.S.S. » Seventeen
Upon Ray III
"The SELF and the *Lotus Illuminator*"

I place my-*SELF*,

In the Lord's Investigative Light

Under the Manifesting Evolution

Of the *Lotus Illuminator*.

« F.F. » 17

**« I Am the Lighted Purpose of Activity Itself
and as I am herenow
ONE, in Spirit and matter — I am *healed!* »**

« S.S.S. » Eighteen
Upon Ray IV
"The Self and the *Lord's Trumpet*"

I place my-*SELF*,

In the Lord's Peaceful Light

Under the Arjuna Concord

Of the *Lord's Trumpet*.

« F.F. » 18

« I Am *two Lights merged as one* within the Hidden One and as I grow, *I glow in the Dark,* and emerge from the Cocoon — a Warrior *healed!* »

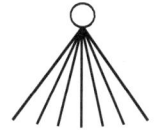

« S.S.S. » Nineteen
Upon Ray V
"The Self and the *Secret Keeper*"

I place my-*Self*,

In the Lord's Silent Light

Under the Concrete Mastership

Of the *Secret Keeper*.

« F.F. » 19

« I Am the Light of Initiation blazing in the full Light of Day and as the One Mind scientifically synthesizing *the minor three*, I know myself as Whole — and am *healed!* »

« S.S.S. » Twenty
Upon Ray VI
"The Self and the *Crucified Lord*"

I place my-*Self*,

In the Lord's Serene Light

Under the Desireless Tutorship

Of the *Crucified Lord*.

« F.F. » 20

« I am the Light of Desire upon the Mountaintop
of Aspiration and from the Divine Heights
of my beloved Light of Lights,
I behold the Clear Vision *that* — I am *healed!* »

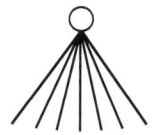

« S.S.S. » Twenty-one
Upon Ray VII
"The SELF and the *Expression of God's Will*"

I place my-*SELF*,

In the Lord's Vivifying Light

Under the Unitive Rhythm

Of the *Expression of God's Will*.

« F.F. » 21

« The lowly light of myself meets the High Light of my-Self and at that Point of *Implosive Convergence* my Shining regenerates the earth — and I am *healed!* »

Three Progressions of **"Light Blessings"** for the **Child**
upon Each of the Seven Cosmic-Physical Rays

... with the addition of

"Born Within Thee" and *"This Suffering Child"* Codicil

Progression I
"In Him Burns Bright the Light"

Bless Thou the child, for in him burns *bright*, the Light of **FIRST LIFE**.

Bless Thou the child, for in him burns *bright*, the Light of **IMMORTAL SOUL**.

Bless Thou the child, for in him burns *bright*, the Light of **ORIGINAL MIND**.

Bless Thou the child, for in him burns *bright*, the Light of **OPEN RELATIONS**.

Bless Thou the child, for in him burns *bright*, the Light of **FRESH OBSERVATION**.

Bless Thou the child, for in him burns *bright*, the Light of **HIGH IDEALISM**.

Bless Thou the child, for in him burns *bright*, the Light of **PURE MAGIC**.

Progression II
"In Him Is Borne Lightly the Light"

Bless Thou the child, for in him is borne *lightly*, the Light of **HARMLESS MIGHT**.

Bless Thou the child, for in him is borne *lightly*, the Light of **NATURAL COMPASSION**.

Bless Thou the child, for in him is borne *lightly*, the Light of **ADAPTIVE INTELLIGENCE**.

Bless Thou the child, for in him is borne *lightly*, the Light of **HOPEFUL STRUGGLE**.

Bless Thou the child, for in him is borne *lightly*, the Light of **ONGOING INVESTIGATION**.

Bless Thou the child, for in him is borne *lightly*, the Light of **FAITHFUL DEVOTION**.

Bless Thou the child, for in him is borne *lightly*, the Light of **CREATIVE THOUGHT**.

Progression III
"Indeed, He was Born Out of the Light"

Bless Thou the child, for *in-deed,* he was born out of the Light of **THY INTENDED WILL.**

Bless Thou the child, for *in-deed,* he was born out of the Light of **THY WISENED LOVE.**

Bless Thou the child, for *in-deed,* he was born out of the Light of **THY PURPOSEFUL ACTIVITY.**

Bless Thou the child, for *in-deed,* he was born out of the Light of **THY INSPIRED SONG.**

Bless Thou the child, for *in-deed,* he was born out of the Light of **THY SCIENTIFIC KNOWLEDGE.**

Bless Thou the child, for *in-deed,* he was born out of the Light of **THY PROVIDENTIAL VISION.**

Bless Thou the child, for *in-deed,* he was born out of the Light of **THY CRYSTALLIZED COGNITION.**

Born Within Thee
To Become Through Thee

(Lord), bless Thou the Child, for he was born *within Thee* to become *through Thee*:

> the World Savior,
> the World Server,
> the Initiate (of the Fifth Kingdom),
> the Individualized Cosmic Christ,
> the Liberated One,
> the Triumphant Disciple, and
> the Adi Adept.

"This Suffering Child"
Codicil

(Lord), bless Thou *this* suffering child come from Thee... (state the *Child's* given Name)...
And by the Grace of Thy Great Being and Thy Compassionate Heart and Thy Palm of Baraka,
May he... (repeat the *Child's* Name) ... be tended to by Thee, and deeply Healed and made Whole again,
(in just accord with the Ring-pass-not of his present karma and future destiny).

So may it be!

Magnificent Magus Publications

Magnificent Magus Publications©
1206 Saint-Luc Boulevard, Suite 110
Saint-Jean-sur-Richelieu, Québec, J2Y 1A5, Canada
info@palmpublications.com
www.palmpublications.com